Daily Life in ANCIENT EGYPT

Don Nardo

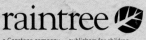

raintree

a Capstone company — publishers for children

Raintree is an imprint of Capstone Global Library Limited, a company incorporated in England and Wales having its registered office at 7 Pilgrim Street, London, EC4V 6LB – Registered company number: 6695582

www.raintreepublishers.co.uk
myorders@raintreepublishers.co.uk

Edited by Clare Lewis
Designed by Philippa Jenkins
Original illustrations © Capstone Global Library Limited 2015
Illustrated by HL Studios, Witney, Oxon
Picture research by Jo Miller
Production by Helen McCreath
Originated by Capstone Global Library Ltd
Printed and bound in China

ISBN 978 1 406 28807 0 (hardback)
18 17 16 15 14
10 9 8 7 6 5 4 3 2 1

ISBN 978 1 406 28813 1 (paperback)
19 18 17 16 15
10 9 8 7 6 5 4 3 2 1

British Library Cataloguing in Publication Data
A full catalogue record for this book is available from the British Library.

Acknowledgements
We would like to thank the following for permission to reproduce photographs: Alamy: age fotostock Spain, S.L., 23, Chronicle, 36, Mary Evans Picture Library, 7, Superstock, 37, Werner Otto, 32, World History Archive, 17, 25; Corbis: Gian Berto Vann, 38, Gianni Dagli Orti, 33; Getty Images: De Agostini Picture Library/M. Carrieri, 27, Hulton Fine Art Collection/Print Collector, 28; Glow Images: Heritage Images/Art Media, 6, Heritage Images/Werner Forman Archive, 26, National Geographic Image Collection/H.M. Herget, 8; Newscom: akg-images, 41, Dallas and John Heaton Stock Conneciton USA, 24, 42, Prisma/Album, 14, 18, Robert Harding Productions, 13, Werner Forman/akg-images, 21, 22, 35, World History Archive, 30; Science Source: Getty Research Institute, 16; Shutterstock: cobalt88, 5, irisphoto1, 40, jsp, 10, Nomad_Soul, 34, PlusONE, 39; SuperStock: Hemis.fr, cover
Design Elements: Nova Development Corporation, clip art (throughout), Shutterstock: imanolqs

We would like to thank Dr Martin Bommas for his help in the preparation of this book.

Every effort has been made to contact copyright holders of material reproduced in this book. Any omissions will be rectified in subsequent printings if notice is given to the publisher.

All the Internet addresses (URLs) given in this book were valid at the time of going to press. However, due to the dynamic nature of the Internet, some addresses may have changed, or sites may have changed or ceased to exist since publication. While the author and publisher regret any inconvenience this may cause readers, no responsibility for any such changes can be accepted by either the author or the publisher.

CONTENTS

Some words are shown in bold, **like this**. You can find out what they mean by looking in the glossary.

People have long been fascinated by ancient Egypt. Over 5,000 years ago, the Egyptians built an amazing **civilization**. We know a lot about the Egyptians' lives from tombs as well as written sources.

A Greek historian, Herodotus, who visited Egypt around 2,500 years ago, called the Egyptian civilization the "gift of the Nile". The Nile is the river that flows from south to north for 6,646 kilometres (4,130 miles), dividing Egypt in two.

The Nile's waters overflowed its banks once a year. It laid down a layer of new soil that made the land around it extremely **fertile**. A variety of crops grew in that narrow strip of land bordering the river.

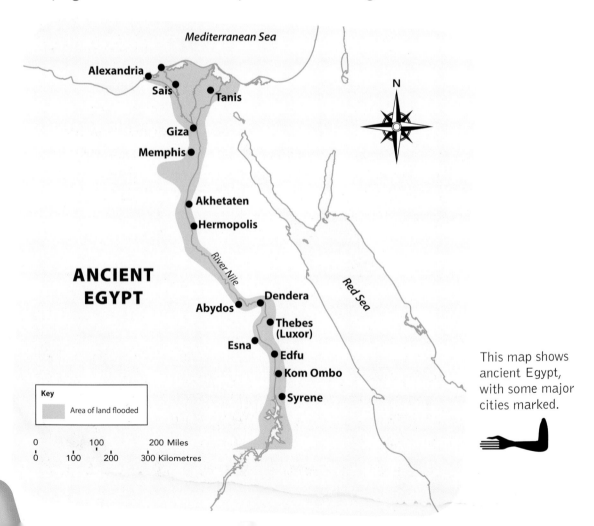

Mediterranean Sea

Alexandria
Sais
Tanis
Giza
Memphis
Akhetaten
Hermopolis

ANCIENT EGYPT

River Nile

Dendera
Abydos
Thebes (Luxor)
Esna
Edfu
Kom Ombo
Syrene

Red Sea

N

Key

Area of land flooded

| 0 | | 100 | | 200 Miles |
| 0 | 100 | 200 | 300 Kilometres | |

This map shows ancient Egypt, with some major cities marked.

Many of Egypt's amazing constructions can still be seen today.

Much of Egypt is dry desert. No one could live in this wasteland. However, in the land next to the Nile, the great cities of Memphis and Thebes grew and flourished. The Nile provided more than drinking water and food. Egyptians also bathed and washed their clothes in its waters. They used the mud on its banks to build their houses. And the river provided a means of transporting goods and people. This included huge stone blocks used to build temples and pyramids.

HOW DO WE KNOW?

Herodotus

Much of what we know about ancient Egypt in the mid-400s comes from a book written by Herodotus - *The Histories*. In it, among other things, he described the Nile's annual flooding. "The country is converted into a sea," he said. "The towns, which alone remain above water, look like islands."

In ancient Egypt, people's homes were very different depending on how rich or poor they were. A small number of people were very wealthy. Richest of all was the king, called the **pharaoh**. He lived in several palaces around the country and had hundreds of servants.

A few thousand nobles were also rich and had large houses and many servants. Most of their homes had bathrooms and toilets. Modern-style plumbing did not exist, however. Instead, a person sat on a wooden or polished stone toilet seat. A pottery container rested below it. A servant emptied the pot outside.

Date palms and other plants thrive in one of several inner courtyards in a pharaoh's palace. Palaces like this were Egypt's biggest homes.

But home life was very different for most other Egyptians. The houses of farmers, fishermen, craftsmen and labourers were very small. The poorest homes had only one room. So the family had to sleep, eat and do almost everything else there. People also kept their goats in their bedroom to keep them safe. The goats' body heat also helped to keep the room warmer on chilly nights. Poorer homes had no bathroom or toilet.

A noble's country home lies amongst large well-kept gardens. The man is using a simple water-lifting device called a shaduf.

COUNTRY VILLAS

Many wealthy Egyptians had large, comfortable country houses. They were often surrounded by vegetable and flower gardens, fruit trees and stables for donkeys and other animals.

Building materials and rooms

The houses of both rich and poor had something in common. They were built from the same materials. Most common were mud-bricks. People pressed the mud into wooden moulds and left them out in the sun to dry. Builders also used bundled river reeds, wood and plaster. These materials were easily damaged by rain and wind, so all Egyptian houses needed frequent repairs.

Servants and slaves

Some Egyptian households could afford to hire servants. There were two different types of servants. One type was a free person, paid as a labourer. The Egyptians called the other type a *hem*. The *hemw* (say "HEM-oo", the plural of *hem*) were not as free as other servants. A *hem* could be bought and sold, for example. *Hemw* also earned less than normal servants did.

 Only a few of the workers on big building projects like this were 4. Many were farmers who were ordered to work on the building sites for a set period of time.

Household gardens

Many Egyptians, often even the poorer ones, kept household gardens. Some grew vegetables; others grew fruit trees or flowers. The gardens might consist of small open spaces between houses. It was also common to grow plants in clay pots. We know about these gardens because artists depicted them in wall paintings.

The *hemw* are often described as slaves. But they had certain **rights**. That made them different from slaves in most other ancient societies, who had *no* rights. A *hem* not only earned small wages, he or she could also own land and other kinds of property. *Hemw* could also marry anyone they wanted, even non-slaves.

A person became a *hem* in various ways. Some *hemw* were captured during war. Others were criminals who lost some rights as a punishment. Still others were born *hemw* because their parents were.

Whether free or a *hem*, a servant performed unskilled tasks. Some servants were maids, while others ran errands. Servants also cooked, served food, did laundry and helped look after the family's animals and gardens.

Food and drink

The preparation and eating of food were two of the most important parts of home life in Egypt. Thanks to the fertile soil bordering the Nile, the Egyptians grew enormous amounts of it. And people enjoyed a wide variety of fruits, vegetables and foods made from grains.

In this ancient wall painting, the man on the right prepares bread dough in a large mixing bowl. The man on the left checks the loaves as they bake.

Bread ovens

Experts know how the Egyptians baked their bread. This is because several bread ovens have been found in ancient houses. The most common type of oven was a circular pottery shell about 1 metre (3 feet) high. The baker lit a fire on the inside and stuck thin pieces of dough to the oven's outer surface.

The most common of those grains was wheat. It produced the country's **staple food** – bread, or *te*. Some vegetables they ate are still popular today. These include beans, cucumbers, lettuce and onions. In the country's earliest times, figs, dates and grapes were the most common fruits. In later times, peaches became popular, too.

The Egyptians also ate various kinds of meat. It came from animals such as cattle, sheep, goats and several kinds of birds and fish. Herodotus told how "some kinds of fish they eat raw". Often they were "either dried in the sun or salted". The Egyptians ate ducks raw, too, he said. But other sorts of birds and fish "they either roast or boil".

COMMON DRINKS

Egyptian farmers drank a lot of milk from cattle and goats. People who lived in the city more often drank beer, called henqet. It was made from various grains and frequently sweetened with date juice or spices.

As it is today, marriage was common among the ancient Egyptians. Some married for love. This is shown by the many surviving love songs and poems. Part of one written by a young woman for her boyfriend reads, "Your love shall endure (last) day and night during the hours when I am asleep and when I wake by day." Most Egyptians, however, got married mainly to have children.

Family marriages

Most Egyptian men married in their late teens. Most women did so between the ages of 12 and 15. Most brides and grooms were not related, but marriages between relatives were not uncommon. Sometimes two cousins got married, for instance. However, marriages between brothers and sisters were rare. But in royal families the practice of marrying close relatives was more common.

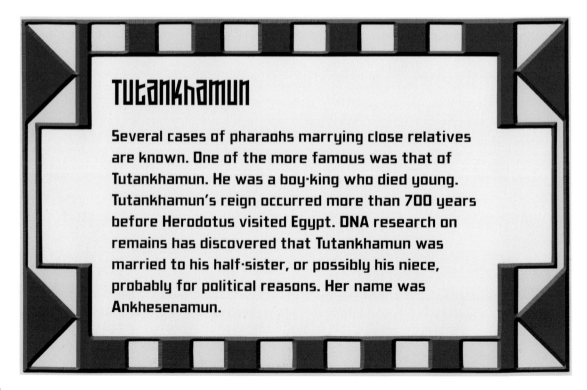

Tutankhamun

Several cases of pharaohs marrying close relatives are known. One of the more famous was that of Tutankhamun. He was a boy-king who died young. Tutankhamun's reign occurred more than 700 years before Herodotus visited Egypt. DNA research on remains has discovered that Tutankhamun was married to his half-sister, or possibly his niece, probably for political reasons. Her name was Ankhesenamun.

 The pharaoh Tutankhamun, often called King Tut for short, appears with his young wife in this ornate carving on the back of his throne.

This small statue found in a tomb shows a priest named Katep and his wife, Hetepheres.

From weddings to divorces

There is little evidence to show exactly how marriages were performed. However, many historians believe that, once a marriage had been arranged, the actual act of getting married was fairly simple. There were no legal papers nor a religious ceremony. The bride and groom were considered married after they moved into their new house together. Ancient wall paintings show wedding parties in which people feasted, sang and danced.

HOW DO WE KNOW?

Egyptian divorce documents

Modern Egyptologists know about a few of the causes of Egyptian divorces. This is largely thanks to an Egyptian law. It required the two people getting divorced to sign an agreement. It stated the reason for the break-up and said that one or both parties were free to remarry. A number of these documents have survived.

It is not known how many Egyptian marriages were successful. It is clear, however, that divorce was not unusual. The reasons that couples broke up were probably similar to those in modern divorces. Most of the time, it was the husband who started the divorce. This may be because of the nature of Egyptian society, which was dominated and largely run by men.

The actual divorce was straightforward. Because most homes were owned by men, the wife was often the one who moved out. Usually, she returned to her parents' home.

Children and education

Most Egyptian couples had at least a few children. However, not all of those born would survive. They did not have access to the quality of medicine we have today. And many children died either during birth or of disease before the age of three.

Children played with wooden toys, such as this rider and horses.

HOW DO WE KNOW?

Common children's toys

Historians know what toys Egyptian children played with. This is partly because those objects are shown in ancient paintings. Also, some of the actual toys survived inside tombs. Many of those toys are similar to modern ones. They include dolls, balls, miniature swords and chariots, and dogs, cats, donkeys and other animals made of wood or clay.

Those children who survived played with toys just as modern children do. But the period during which children could play and just be children was often much shorter than it is today. This was because most children came from poorer homes. So as soon as they were able, they had to start helping their parents make ends meet. Usually no later than the age of ten, boys began learning their fathers' trades and girls started to help their mothers cook, clean and make clothes.

Children from wealthy homes

It was very different for children from wealthier homes. Some of their parents could read and write. Those who could taught their children these skills at an early age.

Many boys from wealthier homes continued their education in formal schools. Their teachers were **scribes**, experts in reading and writing. Classes were held in rooms inside religious buildings or the homes of the pupils' parents.

This limestone statue shows a scribe writing on papyrus, a paper-like material made from the papyrus plant.

All Egyptians, whether rich or poor, felt it was vital to be clean. Most people washed their faces and hands each day. They also bathed often and tried to dress neatly at all times.

These pottery containers from ancient Egypt had many uses. One was to carry water home from the river for washing. Others were drinking cups.

Bathing customs

There was one major drawback to this desire to be clean, however. The average Egyptian house had no bathroom. Instead, a person could walk to the river and bathe there, or he or she could have a sponge bath at home. The person would fill a large bowl or jug with river water, and then use a wet cloth to wipe down his or her body. The last step was to empty the dirty water outside. **Archaeologists** have found such bathing bowls. One has a message written on it. "Good health to you when you wash your face," it says. "And let your heart rejoice!"

Bathing in a richer home that had a bathroom was a different experience. The bather stood or sat on the room's hard **ceramic** or stone floor. He or she scrubbed with soap made from a mix of vegetable oil and powdered stone. Meanwhile, servants poured water over the bather. In some cases, they poured it through a basket, creating a sort of shower. The dirty water drained into a clay container, which was emptied by servants later.

UNKNOWN GERMS

The fact that most Egyptians washed often worked in their favour. They did not suspect the existence of germs, so they did not know what caused various diseases. However, by bathing often, they got rid of many germs, which reduced the likelihood of them becoming ill.

Beauty practices and products

For many Egyptians, appearance was as important as cleanliness. Most men shaved their faces. And women, along with some men, plucked their eyebrows. Men and women also used mouthwash-like substances. The most common was natron, a mixture of mineral salts, which was dissolved in water. Natron is still used in some toothpaste today.

Taking good care of their skin was also important to many Egyptians. It was almost always hot and sunny in Egypt, so people's skin was exposed to sunlight for long periods. To help keep skin smooth, people rubbed on lotions. Some were made from the fat of animals, such as sheep and hippos. Other lotions contained oils made from beans, flax and other plants.

SMELLING NICE

The Egyptians believed that their gods smelt lovely! Many people wanted to smell as good as those gods, so deodorants and perfumes were very popular. Poor people rubbed on an ointment made from ground-up herbs and roots. But members of the upper classes could afford costly perfumes. These were made mainly from plants. Some of the best scents came from lilies, roses, cinnamon and almonds.

Make up

Both men and women used a dark liner to help protect against diseases spread by flies. The eyeliner was made by mixing powdered lead with vegetable oil or water. Many people also added a little reddish colour to their cheeks. The blusher was made from rust. Mixing the blusher with animal fat produced lipstick.

This box, from the tomb of a man named Kha and his wife, Merit, contains the make-up and lotions she would need in the **afterlife**.

This shirt is one of the few items of ancient Egyptian clothing that has survived. It can be seen in London's Petrie Museum.

Changing clothing styles

Most Egyptians were also very concerned with their clothes. Even if their clothes were inexpensive, they made sure they were at least clean. Herodotus noted this fact during his visit. He wrote that the Egyptians "make a special point of continually washing their clothes".

A majority of Egyptians wore clothes made from linen. Linen came from the flax plant. Linen garments were usually draped around the body in some manner. Surviving wall paintings and statues found in tombs show that clothing styles changed slightly over time, as they do in modern times. Yet the Egyptians were very traditional, so some styles were always fashionable.

HATS IN EGYPT

Hats were uncommon in Egypt before Greek rulers took over the country in the late 300s BC. The new Greek-style hats had wide brims to block the sun from wearers' eyes. Earlier, members of the royal family wore headdresses called nemes. Made of cloth, the nemes' sides flared outwards.

Early on, men wore a simple apron or kilt that hung to the knee. Women usually wore a tube dress sewn up along one side. After about 1500 **BC**, wealthy men began wearing linen shirts and tunics over their kilts. Upper-class women also wore a tunic at this time. Their dresses had fringes and other decorations.

These Egyptian sandals, made from plant fibre, date from the Ptolemaic period (332-30 BC), when Egypt was ruled by Greek pharaohs.

In Egypt, whatever a person's job, he or she was not paid in money. Instead, in return for doing a job, a worker received goods. A craftsman was often paid in grain, for example. This exchange of goods for other goods is called the barter system.

Farmers and craftworkers

Farming was the most common job in Egypt. Greek historian Diodorus Siculus visited Egypt in the first century BC. The farmers there, he said, were experts on "the condition of the soil, the flow of the water, the correct time of sowing and reaping".

This painting was discovered in a tomb. It shows a servant working in the Valley of the Kings.

EGYPTIAN PAINTING

Egyptian painters created beautiful pictures on the walls of palaces and tombs. And they followed certain special, sometimes odd rules. One was to make important people, like the pharaoh, look larger than ordinary people. Many paintings show a person's body from the front, while showing his face and legs from the side.

Craftsmen were divided into many separate craft specialists, including potters, tailors, goldsmiths, jewellers, carpenters, stonemasons and glass-makers. The Egyptians saw painters, sculptors and other artists as ordinary craftsmen, too. Most craftsmen did their jobs in large workshops, which were similar to modern factories.

Government officials

Although the pharaoh was in charge of government, he did not run it on a daily basis. That was the job of his **vizier**, or chief administrator. Most government officials belonged to the upper classes. Only rarely did a lower-class Egyptian climb the social ladder and become a scribe or minister.

This carving shows a potter making clay pots on a wheel.

Weni

One uncommon case of a peasant gaining fame and fortune was that of Weni. Weni started out as an ordinary soldier. But he was talented and worked extra hard, so he rose through the ranks. He became a high government official during the late 2000s BC.

A soldier's life

Working as a soldier was an important job in ancient Egypt. Because Weni began as a soldier, he provided some crucial facts about that occupation. Many soldiers were the sons of soldiers. Often when a soldier died in battle or retired, his son took his place.

Other young men joined the army because they wanted to obtain **booty**. After conquering an enemy town, a military general took livestock, jewellery and other valuables. Often he gave some of this booty to his soldiers. Another advantage of soldiering was to win medals for courage.

Although soldiering had certain benefits, it also had a number of drawbacks. During military campaigns, for instance, marches were long and hard. And the risk of dying in battle was a real threat. Being a soldier could also mean long months away from home and family.

Horses were used by soldiers and hunters to pull chariots.

Egyptian soldiers, as well as mercenaries (soldiers who fought for pay rather than loyalty to a leader) had a high risk of dying in battle.

DO NOT BECOME A SOLDIER!

The hardships and dangers of being a soldier are listed in a document written by an Egyptian scribe. The following passage is meant to be amusing. But the author was serious about discouraging his pupils from becoming soldiers. A soldier's drinking water, the scribe warns, "is smelly and tastes of salt". Also, soldiers often come down with painful illnesses. Moreover, the scribe says, even if the army wins a battle, some soldiers are killed, so they never return to their homes. And even if a soldier survives, the poor fellow "is worn out from marching"!

The Egyptians spent a lot of time and energy on tombs, mummies and other aspects of death and the afterlife. So many early modern writers thought they were obsessed with death.

Like everybody, the Egyptians did have their serious side. But they balanced it with a happy, fun-loving side. "It is hateful to the spirit to be robbed of the time for merriment," one high-placed Egyptian said. These words are confirmed by his people's love for all sorts of leisure activities.

This image is from the tomb of a man called Nebamun. It shows a scene from the afterlife.

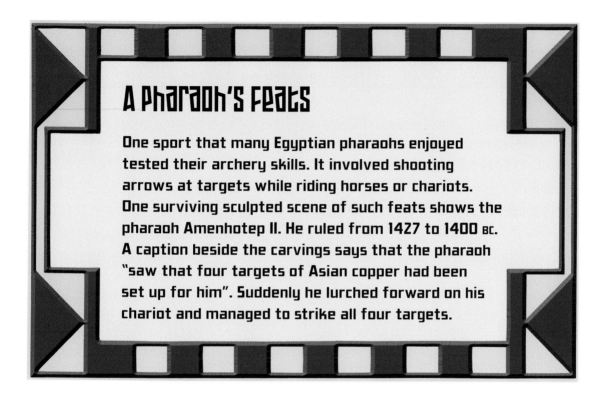

A Pharaoh's Feats

One sport that many Egyptian pharaohs enjoyed tested their archery skills. It involved shooting arrows at targets while riding horses or chariots. One surviving sculpted scene of such feats shows the pharaoh Amenhotep II. He ruled from 1427 to 1400 BC. A caption beside the carvings says that the pharaoh "saw that four targets of Asian copper had been set up for him". Suddenly he lurched forward on his chariot and managed to strike all four targets.

Games of the rich and famous

Pharaohs and other wealthy people enjoyed some activities that poorer people did not. Often this was because these pastimes were very expensive, so ordinary people could not afford them.

One example was large-scale hunting expeditions. The king and some nobles set out with servants, traps and hunting dogs. If they planned to stay out overnight, they also took along huge tents. These tents had all sorts of luxuries, including comfortable beds.

Board games

Many Egyptians enjoyed playing board games. The most popular game was senet. The game board had a grid of squares and a number of small game pieces. These pieces were similar in some ways to those in modern chess and draughts. Poor people usually could not afford the proper boards and game pieces. They simply scratched a grid on the surface of a flat stone and used little rocks or bones as game pieces. A number of senet sets have survived. But so far, experts have not worked out the game's exact rules.

Queen Nefertiti, wife of the warrior pharaoh Ramesses II, plays the board game senet in this painting found in her tomb.

The Egyptians played several other board games. One, known as mehen, involved up to six players. Its game pieces were shaped like dogs, lions and balls. Unfortunately, like senet, its rules remain unknown.

Ball games

Ball games were also popular in ancient Egypt, particularly among children. Many of those games are shown in surviving paintings. In a scene painted on a tomb's wall, some children juggle several balls at once. Another painting shows two girls throwing a small ball back and forth. Standing nearby, their friends clap their hands, apparently providing a beat for the throws. Other ball games featured dance steps.

HOW DO WE KNOW?

Evidence for senet

Archaeologists discovered four sets of senet boards and game pieces in Tutankhamun's tomb. And they found several other sets in other tombs. A number of surviving paintings show the game, too. One created in about 1150 BC shows an antelope and lion playing senet!

These pictures of wrestlers were found at Beni Hasan (see box). In the contest in the centre of the top row, one fighter tries to trip the other.

Wrestling

The Egyptians also greatly enjoyed wrestling. Historians now know that it was the oldest and most popular sport of the ancient world. Moreover, many of its moves were the same or very similar to those of modern wrestling.

Young boys learned to wrestle partly by watching older relatives and friends. They also took part in matches in their villages. It was similar to the way children play football in the garden today. Some of the best wrestlers entertained the pharaoh and royal court. A surviving sculpture shows such a match. One wrestler chokes the other, and an attached caption suggests this was against the rules. It reads: "Take care! You are in the presence of the Pharaoh!"

HOW DO WE KNOW?

Egyptian wrestling moves

Most ancient Egyptian wrestling moves are well known. This is because a large collection of paintings of wrestlers has survived. There are more than 400 detailed scenes in all. They were discovered at Beni Hasan, in Middle (central) Egypt. The pictures also reveal that referees oversaw the matches.

Men also played a water sport where they stood on a boat, armed with poles, and tried to knock men on another boat into the water.

Water sports

Water sports were nearly as popular as wrestling in Egypt. This was probably due to the mighty Nile's importance in the country. Many people enjoyed swimming, for example. And fishing and boat races were common pastimes for richer people.

Another popular water sport was a lot riskier than the others. It involved taking a small boat into the river's rapids. These were places where the water was very choppy and dangerous. According to an eyewitness, these vessels were "violently tossed about". Swept along "by the whole force of the river", they would "plunge head downward to the great terror of the onlookers".

Religion and rituals were central to the Egyptians' life. And many of their social **customs** involved preparation for death and the journey to the afterlife.

A god for every occasion

The Egyptians worshipped many gods. Most people believed that almost everything that happened in the world was caused by one god or another. One god caused storms, for instance. Hundreds of gods were recognized across Egypt. But most were minor and were worshipped mainly in local areas. Of the major gods, the sun god, Ra, was especially important. He supposedly travelled across the sky each day, giving the world light and warmth.

Osiris was another important god. He ruled the kingdom of the dead, or Underworld. Osiris's sister and wife, Isis, was seen as a comforting mother figure. And artists often showed her holding her baby son, Horus.

This modern depiction shows Ra as a hawk-headed man. Here, he holds an ankh, representing life, in his right hand. The sceptre in his left hand is a symbol of power.

This wall painting shows Osiris-Ra as a ram-headed man. The goddesses Nephthys (left) and Isis stand beside him.

WINNING OVER OSIRIS

Every Egyptian hoped to enjoy eternity in the afterlife after death. But to enter Osiris's kingdom, one first had to win that god's favour. So many people memorized some special phrases to say to Osiris at the crucial moment. One was: "I have not committed evil against men." Another stated, "I have not killed anyone."

The Myth of Kingship

One of Egypt's many spiritual ideas was a **myth** known as the Contending of Horus and Seth. It featured Osiris, Isis, their divine brother Seth and their son Horus. The tale told how the nation's line of kings was established.

Long ago, it began, Osiris was Egypt's king. Seth came to resent his brother and killed him. Then he cut up the body, hid the pieces and seized the throne. Outraged, Isis searched for and found the bloody pieces. She used her magic to bring Osiris back to life. And not long afterwards, she gave birth to their child, Horus.

In this more modern painting, Isis shows off her baby son, Horus.

This family portrait was made from gold. It shows Osiris (middle). The hawk-headed Horus (left) and Isis stand beside him.

After Horus grew into a young man, he challenged Seth's right to the throne. The two gods fought fiercely. Horus won. He became pharaoh – the last of Egypt's god-kings. Thereafter, human pharaohs ruled, and each carried part of Horus's spirit. Moreover, when a pharaoh died, his spirit joined with that of Horus's father, Osiris.

The Myth of Kingship taught the Egyptians that each dead pharaoh was part god, so those kings were worthy of worship. For that reason, the government built special temples dedicated to dead kings. The temples' priests prayed that the pharaohs would do well in the afterlife.

Many sacred rituals

Most rituals of ancient Egyptian religion were intended to keep the gods happy. People believed that bad human behaviour angered the gods. And if angry enough, those gods might destroy the world. It was therefore important to stay on the gods' good sides. The key to doing that was to carry out the religious rituals regularly.

Of these acts, the main ones were prayer and offerings meant to please the gods. One common kind of offering was one in which the corpses of preserved animals, such as cats, dogs, monkeys and birds, were placed inside tombs or vaults in honour of a god or gods.

These men are preparing a cow for sacrifice. They killed the animal, carefully butchered it and burned selected parts on the altar.

The Egyptians performed many other religious rituals. Priests carefully looked after **sacred** statues in temples. And the public attended annual festivals that honoured the gods. Those celebrations featured prayer, sacred **processions** and feasts.

Mummification

Other rituals were also carried out to ensure that dead people achieved the afterlife. One was mummification, or **embalming**. Its purpose was to preserve the body during its journey to Osiris's kingdom and in the afterlife. The embalmers removed the internal organs. Then they dried the remains and wrapped them in cloth. Those families that could afford it placed the mummies in brick or stone tombs. They also buried **grave goods** – food, tools and other objects – with the body. People believed the dead would use them in the afterlife.

PYRAMIDS AT GIZA

The pharaohs could afford the most splendid tombs. The biggest and most famous are the three pyramids at Giza, near modern Cairo. It took thousands of workers to build these huge tombs. Deep inside each pyramid was a chamber that held the king's remains. When they were first built, the pyramids were covered in smooth polished stone that shone in the sun.

The highly traditional Egyptians maintained their unique way of life for more than 2,000 years. But beginning in about 1069 BC, civil strife and other troubles weakened the country. In 674 BC the Assyrians, from what is now Iraq, invaded Egypt. Other foreign conquerors followed. The Persians arrived in 525 BC. Then came the Greeks in 332 BC. Finally, in 30 BC, Egypt became a Roman province. It remained so until Rome fell in **AD** 476.

The Romans and later foreigners who controlled Egypt were fascinated by Egyptian culture. Rome, for example, adopted several Egyptian gods and myths. The famous battle between Horus and Seth is an example. Some historians think it was the model for the medieval story of St George and the dragon.

ANCIENT EGYPT IN LAS VEGAS

People are still fascinated by ancient Egypt today. For example, the Luxor Hotel in Las Vegas, USA, has been built in an Egyptian style. It even has a 30-storey pyramid!

The Last Pharaoh

Many people think of Queen Cleopatra when they think of ancient Egypt. She was the last active pharaoh, before Egypt was conquered by the Romans. The story says that she poisoned herself after suffering defeat by allowing a poisonous snake to bite her. Her life and dramatic death have inspired plays, stories and movies.

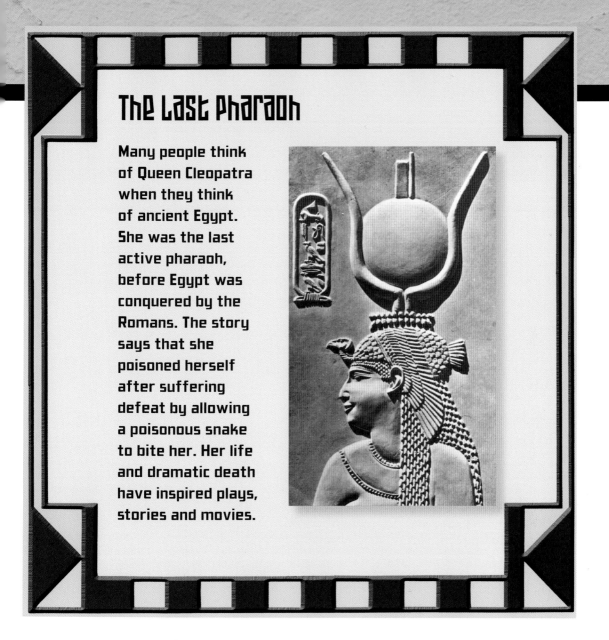

In early modern times, Europeans and Americans were attracted to Egypt in a different way. Archaeologists and historians began to uncover its ancient secrets. Images of mummies, giant pyramids and hidden tombs made Egypt fascinating to people across the globe. And various Egyptian artefacts were collected and put on display in museums around the world.

As a result, artists of all kinds were, and still are, inspired to recapture Egyptian life. They produced poems, operas, paintings, books and films with Egyptian themes.

A day in the life of an Egyptian child

My name is Seti. I am ten years old. I yawn and stretch as I awake to the early morning sun. Last night, to keep cool, my family and I slept on reed mats on the flat roof of our home.

I quickly wash and dress in my white linen shirt, then join my older sister and younger brother for breakfast of bread and fruit. We sit on the floor to eat it. Our father sits on the stool.

My father is a farmer and has a hard day's work ahead of him in the fields. The harvest has done well this year, though, so first he must take some of the wheat to the temple as payment for using temple land. He loads the wheat onto his donkey and sets off.

It is laundry day so my mother gathers the linen bed sheets and takes them down to the riverbanks. We go with her. My brother and I paddle while my mother and sister rub the washing against a large stone in the river until it is clean. Then they lie it out in the sun to dry. While we wait, I play senet with my friend in the sand.

Once the clothes are dry, I help my mother carry the sheets and a waterpot full of water back home for cooking and washing.

At home, we have a lunch of bread and lettuce. There is no meat to eat today. My sister is to be married soon so perhaps we will have meat on the wedding day.

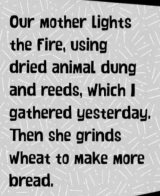

Our mother lights the fire, using dried animal dung and reeds, which I gathered yesterday. Then she grinds wheat to make more bread.

When our father comes home, mother serves a vegetable dish. We scoop the stew up with bread and eat with our fingers.

At 6pm it is already dark outside. My family and I go to sleep, ready for another early wake-up in the morning.

TIMELINE

4000 BC
Egyptian farmers start to take advantage of the River Nile's yearly floods

3100 BC
The first pharaoh, Narmer, unifies Upper and Lower Egypt. To celebrate his achievements, he builds a new capital city at Memphis, just south of the Nile Delta.

2667–2648 BC
Egypt's royal architect, Imhotep, designs and builds the world's first large stone structure, the Step Pyramid at Sakkara

2589–2566 BC
Pharaoh Khufu's pyramid, the largest ever produced in Egypt, is built at Giza, near modern-day Cairo

2320 BC
A former soldier named Weni serves as vizier to the pharaoh Pepy I.

2060–1991 BC
The Egyptians build a new capital city at Thebes, in Upper Egypt

1550–1069 BC
Years of the New Kingdom, in which a series of strong pharaohs create an Egyptian empire stretching well into Palestine

1427–1400 BC
Reign of the pharaoh Amenhotep II, known for performing various athletic feats

1352–1336 BC
Reign of the pharaoh Akhenaton, who rejects the traditional gods and promotes the worship of a single god, Aten

1336–1327 BC
Tutankhamun is Egypt's pharaoh

1274 BC
The warrior pharaoh Ramesses II wins a major victory over the Hittites (from Anatolia, what is now Turkey) near Kadesh, in southern Syria

1174 BC
The pharaoh Ramesses III defeats enemies in northern Egypt

1069 BC
The final year of the period of Egypt's height of power, after which the country begins to weaken

674 BC
The Assyrians conquer Egypt

525 BC
The Persians take over Egypt

455–450 BC
The Greek historian Herodotus visits Egypt and includes a great deal of information about the country in what will later be seen as the world's first true history book

332 BC
A Greek army led by Alexander the Great enters Egypt

323 BC
Alexander unexpectedly dies and his generals fight over his empire. One of those successors, Ptolemy, seizes Egypt and establishes a family line of Greek rulers there.

60 BC
The Greek historian Diodorus Siculus travels to Egypt

51 BC
Cleopatra VII, last of the Greek Ptolemaic rulers of Egypt, becomes pharaoh

31 BC
After teaming up with Roman general Mark Antony, Cleopatra is defeated at Actium, in Greece, and soon afterwards kills herself. This marks the passing of Egypt's last pharaoh.

30 BC
The Romans turn Egypt into part of their empire

GLOSSARY

AD short for *anno domini* - after the birth of Jesus Christ

afterlife life after death

archaeologist scientist who digs up and studies past civilizations

BC before the birth of Jesus Christ

booty valuables that the winner of a battle takes from the loser

ceramic made of clay or pottery

civilization society with culture, laws and government and written language

custom way of acting that is usual for people in a particular culture

embalming treating a dead body in ways that will protect or preserve it

fertile able to produce plants such as farm crops

grave goods food, tools and other useful objects placed in a grave or tomb for the use of the dead person in the afterlife

myth old story, often religious in nature, based on legend

pharaoh royal ruler of ancient Egypt

procession religious parade

rights something owed to a person by law

sacred special for religious reasons

scribe person who makes a living through the ability to read and write

staple food nutritious food widely common to a people, region, or country

vizier in ancient Egypt, the pharaoh's chief administrator and advisor

Books

Ancient Egypt (History Detective Investigates), Rachel Minay (Wayland, 2014)
Egypt (Discover Countries), Camilla de la Bedoyere (Wayland, 2012)
The Curse of King Tut's Tomb (Graphic History), Michael Burgan (Raintree, 2011)
What Did the Ancient Egyptians Do for Me?, Patrick Catel (Raintree, 2011)

Websites

www.ancientegypt.co.uk/geography/home.html
This website, created by the British Museum, has lots of information and a section where you can explore different maps of Egypt.

www.childrensuniversity.manchester.ac.uk/interactives/history/egypt
Find out lots of information about ancient Egypt on the Children's University of Manchester's website.

www.pbs.org/wgbh/nova/ancient/explore-ancient-egypt.html
This excellent interactive PBS site allows the reader to explore ancient Egypt as if he or she is actually there.

www.schoolsliaison.org.uk/kids/access/egypt/mummies_egypt.htm
Click on each mummy here and find out all sorts of facts about some real Egyptian mummies.

Places to visit

The British Museum, London
www.britishmuseum.org
Visit the British Museum to see many objects from ancient Egypt.

The Manchester Museum, Manchester
www.museum.manchester.ac.uk
The Manchester Museum has one of the largest collections of Egyptian artefacts in the UK

INDEX